CALVIN SPANN

DARING FIGHTER PILOT

BY DUCHESS HARRIS, JD, PHD

WITH SAMANTHA S. BELL

Core Library

An Imprint of Abdo Publishing
abdobooks.com

Cover image: Calvin Spann was an African American
fighter pilot in the 1940s.

abdobooks.com

Published by Abdo Publishing, a division of ABDO, PO Box 398166, Minneapolis, Minnesota 55439. Copyright © 2020 by Abdo Consulting Group, Inc. International copyrights reserved in all countries. No part of this book may be reproduced in any form without written permission from the publisher. Core Library™ is a trademark and logo of Abdo Publishing.

Printed in the United States of America, North Mankato, Minnesota
092019
012020

Cover Photo: Private Collection of Lt. Calvin J. Spann/United States Army Air Corps/ Wikimedia Commons
Interior Photos: Private Collection of Lt. Calvin J. Spann/United States Army Air Corps/Wikimedia Commons, 1; Bill Crump/Alamy, 5, 43; Circa Images/Newscom, 6–7, 9; Buyenlarge/Archive Photos/ Getty Images, 12–13; PhotoQuest/Archive Photos/Getty Images, 16; Everett Collection/Newscom, 18, 28–29; Bettmann/Getty Images, 20–21; Afro American Newspapers/Gado/Archive Photos/ Getty Images, 22, 24; Red Line Editorial, 26, 37; World History Archive/Newscom, 31; Lev Radin/ Shutterstock Images, 34–35; Chuck Kennedy/MCT/Newscom, 39

Editor: Maddie Spalding
Series Designer: Ryan Gale

Library of Congress Control Number: 2019941998

Publisher's Cataloging-in-Publication Data

Names: Harris, Duchess, author. | Bell, Samantha S., author.
Title: Calvin Spann: daring fighter pilot / by Duchess Harris and Samantha S. Bell
Other title: daring fighter pilot
Description: Minneapolis, Minnesota : Abdo Publishing, 2020 | Series: Freedom's promise | Includes online resources and index.
Identifiers: ISBN 9781532190797 (lib. bdg.) | ISBN 9781532176647 (ebook)
Subjects: LCSH: Spann, Calvin J.--Juvenile literature. | Fighter pilots--United States-- Biography--Juvenile literature. | African American fighter pilots--Biography--Juvenile literature. | World War, 1939-1945--Juvenile literature. | United States. Air Force-- African Americans--Biography--Juvenile literature. | Tuskegee Airmen, Inc.-- Juvenile literature.
Classification: DDC 940.5449730 [B]--dc23

CONTENTS

A LETTER FROM DUCHESS

Many young people have heard of the Tuskegee Airmen. This book will give you insight into the life of one of these great men: Calvin Spann. Spann was a hero because he fought for the United States. He was a pilot at a time when the US military was segregated. Black service members had to train and fight in separate units from white service members. Black pilots received training at Tuskegee Army Air Field in Alabama. They were called the Tuskegee Airmen.

Like other Tuskegee Airmen, Spann was sent abroad to fight during World War II. He participated in 26 missions. After the war, he tried to become a commercial pilot. But airlines would not accept Black pilots. Despite this discrimination, Spann continued to build a successful life and career. He shared the story of the Tuskegee Airmen. He was a role model to young people. We can preserve the legacy of the Tuskegee Airmen by sharing their stories in turn.

Please join me on a journey that explores the life of Calvin Spann. His career in World War II has helped younger generations enjoy the freedom of flight.

Duchess Harris

Calvin Spann was one of the 355 Tuskegee Airmen who served abroad during World War II.

THE LONGEST FLIGHT

In March 1945, Lieutenant Calvin Spann received the orders for his next mission. The United States was fighting Germany, Italy, and Japan in World War II (1939–1945). Spann was one of the Tuskegee Airmen. The airmen were the first African American pilots in the US Army Air Corps. Spann flew with the 332nd Fighter Group, also known as the Red Tails. They flew as escorts for bomber planes.

The Red Tails' new mission was dangerous. They would fly with a group of bombers. In addition to the Red Tails, four other fighter groups would help protect the bombers. The bombers would fly into Berlin, Germany.

Tuskegee Airmen gathered on base before each mission to go over the details of the mission.

BENJAMIN O. DAVIS JR.

Benjamin O. Davis Jr. was an accomplished pilot. He initially trained to be part of the US Army. He graduated from the US Military Academy at West Point in 1936. He was the only Black cadet at the academy. He then taught military science at Tuskegee Institute in Alabama. He attended flying school at Tuskegee in 1941. The school began training Black pilots that year. He became the commander of the Red Tails in 1943. After World War II ended, he continued to serve in the military. In 1998 he became the first African American general in the US Air Force.

Their target was a huge tank factory. The Germans used tanks to help defend the capital city. Destroying the tank factory could help the United States and its allies win the war.

On March 24, the airmen and bombers left their base in Ramitelli, Italy. The airmen's orders were to pass off the bombers to another fighter group when they neared Berlin. But things did not go as planned. The other fighter group did not arrive. The airmen

Before a mission, mechanics had to make sure the airmen's planes were in working order.

needed to save their fuel for the trip back. But they decided to stay with the bombers.

THE BATTLE IN THE AIR

The mission was not easy. Once the American planes entered German territory, their radars did not work well. Also, the Germans flew jets that could shoot down enemy planes and then quickly fly away.

As the group entered Berlin, they encountered German jets. The airmen shot down three jets. The bombers slipped away and bombed the factory.

The airmen had traveled more than 1,600 miles (2,600 km). This was the Red Tails' longest mission.

Most of their planes were nearly out of fuel by the time they returned to their base.

Spann and other Red Tails were honored for their part in the mission. They received the Presidential Unit Citation. This citation is awarded to military units that show heroism.

THE STRUGGLE AT HOME

The airmen had faced many challenges even before entering the war. In the 1940s, Jim Crow laws enforced racial segregation in the United States. Racial segregation is the separation of people into groups based on their race.

Under these laws, African Americans could not use the same facilities or services as white people. The laws also stated that they could not become military pilots.

In September 1940, the White House announced that the military would offer training to African Americans as pilots and mechanics. But they would be segregated into all-Black combat units. They were separated from white recruits during training. An air base in Tuskegee, Alabama, became the center for their training program. The men who trained there would become known as the Tuskegee Airmen.

FURTHER EVIDENCE

Chapter One describes how the Tuskegee Airmen and other African Americans were discriminated against in the 1900s. What was one of the main points of this chapter? What evidence is included to support this point? Read the article and watch the video at the website below. Does the information on the website support the point you identified? Does it present new evidence?

TUSKEGEE AIRMEN
abdocorelibrary.com/calvin-spann

BUILDING CONFIDENCE

Calvin Spann was born in Wallington, New Jersey, on November 28, 1924. He had four sisters and one brother. They grew up in Rutherford, New Jersey. Neighborhoods in the town were segregated.

In junior high school, Calvin began playing football. He was small for his age. He had to play against boys who weighed a lot more. But he was fast and daring. The coaches often chose him to play.

When Calvin was in high school, one of the pastors at his church started a boxing program.

Calvin Spann, *standing, first from right*, became interested in flying at an early age.

Calvin soon became a boxer. He learned a lot through his accomplishments in sports. He was confident that he could do whatever he wanted to do.

A BOXING CHAMPION

Calvin became a boxing champion at a young age. As a boxer, he competed against other boxers in his region. The winners moved on to a national competition. It was called the Golden Gloves Tournament of Champions. Calvin won this tournament when he was just 16 years old.

A DESIRE TO FLY

As a high school student, Calvin loved reading comics. One of his favorite characters was a pilot named Smilin' Jack. Calvin wanted to become a pilot too. His family lived near an airport. He often watched planes take off and fly over his house. He decided that joining the Army Air Corps would be a good way to learn to fly.

In 1940 the United States issued its first peacetime draft. The US government was preparing its military forces in case the United States decided to enter the war. White men between the ages of 21 and 36 had to register for the draft. They could be chosen for military service. Black men were excluded from the draft. Military leaders did not think Black people were capable enough to fight.

In December 1941, Japanese forces attacked a US military base in Pearl Harbor, Hawaii. This prompted the United States to enter the war. But the US military needed more service members. The draft ages were expanded. White men between the ages of 18 and 37 had to register.

A poster of a Tuskegee Airman urged Americans to buy war bonds during World War II. People who bought war bonds helped the military pay for its expenses.

Black men were still passed over for the draft. This changed in 1943. In that year, Black men who were within the draft age were registered. But a quota was put in place. The quota limited the number of Black people who were drafted.

Black service members were assigned to segregated divisions. At first they were only assigned to support roles such as cooking or grave digging. They did hard labor. But they were not allowed to fight. This changed as the war continued. Black men were later allowed to join combat units.

When a man was drafted, he did not get to choose which part of the service he joined. But volunteers who enlisted had more choices. Two of Calvin's older friends were drafted. Calvin decided to enlist so he could join the Army Air Corps. He was only 17 years old and still in high school.

INTO THE SERVICE

Before he could enlist, Calvin had to take an exam. He had to show that he knew enough to cover the first two years of college. The exam tested his knowledge of math and science. Calvin excelled in both subjects. He passed the exam.

Segregation thoroughly separated Black people from white people in the South.

Because he was not yet an adult, Calvin also needed his parents' permission to enlist. Calvin's father had died earlier, when Calvin was 16 years old. He convinced his mother that this was what he wanted to do. She approved.

Calvin was supposed to graduate from high school in June 1943. But in May, he received orders to report to Keesler Army Airfield in Biloxi, Mississippi. He missed the last few weeks of high school. One of his sisters accepted his diploma for him at graduation.

Calvin traveled to Mississippi by train. He had never been outside of New Jersey before. He ate his meals in the dining car. But when the train moved south of Washington, DC, the porters gave Calvin a warning. They told him they would have to pull a curtain around him while he ate. They were worried about white travelers on passing trains. They thought the travelers would see Calvin in the dining car and try to shoot him. This was Calvin's first experience with Jim Crow laws.

Calvin arrived in Biloxi and presented his orders. The officers told him that they did not train African Americans. They gave him a room and a bed. But they did not give him a uniform or any duties. Approximately one week later, Calvin received orders to go to Tuskegee, Alabama. Once there, he would train with other African American cadets.

TRAINING AT TUSKEGEE

Spann and other Black cadets were trained at a school in Tuskegee called Tuskegee Normal and Industrial Institute. Booker T. Washington founded this school in 1881. Washington was an African American educator. The school was one of the first institutions of higher learning for African Americans. At first, the school's focus was on training students to become teachers. But the school and its programs grew throughout the early 1900s. In July 1941, Tuskegee began providing military flight training to African Americans.

An army general speaks to the first class of Tuskegee Airmen, the 99th Pursuit Squadron, at Tuskegee Institute in 1941.

Colonel Noel Parrish, *left*, gives Tuskegee Airmen captains Harold Sawyer, *middle*, and Milton Brooks, *right*, special pins to recognize their service.

Black cadets at Tuskegee Institute completed the same flight school coursework as white cadets on other bases. They studied subjects such as meteorology. They learned how to read navigational instruments. Then they were transferred to the Tuskegee Army Air Field for their flight training.

The Army Air Corps assigned officers to oversee this training. Most of them were white. In 1942 Colonel Noel Parrish began serving as the commander of the airmen. He was white too. He knew that many white people did not support the airmen. But he judged the cadets based on their performance instead of their skin color.

LIFE AT TUSKEGEE

Spann and the other cadets had to pass four phases of flight training. Each phase took approximately nine weeks. Training was challenging. Cadets studied subjects such as physics and navigation.

A TUSKEGEE AIRWOMAN

Mildred Hemmons Carter was a Black female pilot in the 1940s. She trained at the Tuskegee Institute's Civilian Pilot Training Program. She graduated from the program in 1941. Then she earned her pilot's license. She applied to be part of the Women Airforce Service Pilots (WASP). WASP was a group of female civilian pilots. They flew planes between bases. They tested planes. WASP rejected Carter because of her race. But the Army Air Corps hired her. The Air Corps did not offer military flight training to women. But Carter had many important responsibilities. She handled paperwork and maintained parachutes. She even bulldozed trees to create an airstrip.

At Tuskegee, cadets learned how to read maps and plan missions.

Many cadets had come from other parts of the country. They were not used to the Jim Crow laws in the South. Black people encountered segregation in all parts of the country. But segregation and racial violence were most widespread in the South. White people sometimes beat or even killed African Americans for perceived insults. These killings were called lynchings. Most lynchings happened in the South.

Parrish did not want the cadets to be harmed. He encouraged them to stay on the base when they were not training. Instead of going into town for entertainment, the cadets watched movies at the base. They also went to dances at the school.

Spann was in a class with more than 130 other cadets. The military put a quota on the number of cadets that could graduate. In Spann's class, approximately 30 cadets made it through the program. Cadets could be

PERSPECTIVES
SUPPORT FROM THE FIRST LADY

Eleanor Roosevelt was First Lady from 1933 to 1945. She supported African Americans' civil rights. She advocated for better schools for African Americans. She also spoke out against lynching. In 1941 she visited the Tuskegee Army Air Field. She took a flight with one of the pilots. Chief flight instructor Charles Alfred Anderson flew the plane. By flying with a Black pilot, the First Lady showed her support for the Tuskegee Institute's training program. She had a photo taken of the flight. She used it to help convince the president that the airmen should serve overseas.

TUSKEGEE GRADUATES

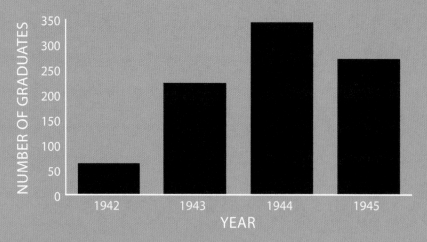

From 1941 to 1946, approximately 1,000 Black pilots trained at Tuskegee Institute. The above graph shows the number of graduates in certain years. Which year had the most graduates? Does this graph help you better understand the influence of the Tuskegee training program?

cut for minor errors. They were expected to meet high standards. Sometimes the air force did not tell cadets why they were cut.

Some of Spann's instructors were harsh or abusive. In some cases, they would insult cadets or hit the cadets' legs with sticks. Despite the pressure and challenges he faced, Spann was determined to make it through the program. Many people thought

African Americans could not learn to fly planes. Spann wanted to prove them wrong.

COMBAT TRAINING

Spann graduated from the program in 1944. Then he moved on to the Walterboro Army Airfield in Walterboro, South Carolina. This was the final training location for the Tuskegee Airmen before they went overseas. In Walterboro, Spann began training for combat. This training lasted three months. The pilots trained every day from dawn until dusk. Spann became a replacement pilot for the 332nd Fighter Group.

EXPLORE ONLINE

Chapter Three discusses the training the airmen received. The article at the website below goes into more depth on this topic. As you know, every source is different. What information does the website give? How is the information from the website the same as the information in Chapter Three? What new information did you learn from the website?

TRAINING
abdocorelibrary.com/calvin-spann

AT THE FRONT

In Europe, most of the US troops were segregated. Some white soldiers formed friendships with their Black comrades. But many discriminated against Black soldiers. In Britain, white soldiers tried to ban Black soldiers from clubs and movie theaters. Sometimes white soldiers were hostile. Some attacked and even killed Black soldiers.

The unit that Spann was assigned to was segregated. Spann became a member of the 100th Fighter Squadron. This squadron was part of the 332nd Fighter Group. The 332nd Fighter Group was an all-Black pilot unit.

African American soldiers arrive in France in 1944. Black troops fought in separate units and faced discrimination in Europe.

THE DOUBLE V CAMPAIGN

While many African Americans served abroad during World War II, others fought another type of battle at home. They were treated as second-class citizens in their own country. Many joined the Double V Campaign. The letter *V* represented victory over the enemy. Campaign activists hoped for both victory in the war and victory in achieving equal rights. They helped with the war effort. Black colleges and universities offered training for Black soldiers. At the same time, activists worked on civil rights issues. They marched and protested for better treatment. They wanted to end segregation and discrimination.

Spann was sent overseas in 1944. He boarded a ship with other airmen in Newport News, Virginia. Their first stop was Marseilles, France. Then they continued on to Naples, Italy. Once there, the men rode trucks through the mountains. Their new base of operations was Ramitelli, Italy.

The airmen flew older planes that white pilots no longer used. These planes were slower and more difficult to

Lieutenant Colonel Benjamin O. Davis Jr. helped lead the Tuskegee Airmen during World War II.

navigate than the enemy German planes. Spann flew as a replacement combat pilot. This meant he did not have his own plane. Instead, he used whatever planes were available.

MISSIONS

Sometimes Spann went on reconnaissance, or recon, missions. During these missions, the pilot of the recon plane took photos of enemy activity on the ground. This was a fast way to get information about the enemy.

Two escort planes went with the recon plane. The three planes had to fly at low altitudes above the treetops. This way, they could fly below the enemy's radar and get better pictures.

The 332nd Fighter Group flew its last combat mission on April 26, 1945. Two weeks later, the Germans surrendered. Spann had completed 26 missions by the time the war ended. The Tuskegee Airmen had flown more than 15,000 missions. Sixty-six airmen died in combat.

STRAIGHT TO THE
SOURCE

In 1942 James G. Thompson wrote a letter to the editor of the Black newspaper the *Pittsburgh Courier*. Thompson was an African American man from Kansas. In his letter, he wrote:

> *Being an American of dark complexion and some 26 years, these questions flash through my mind: "Should I sacrifice my life to live half American?" "Will things be better for the next generation in the peace to follow?" "Would it be . . . too much to demand full citizenship rights in exchange for the sacrificing of my life?" "Is the kind of America I know worth defending?" . . . "Will Colored Americans suffer still the indignities that have been heaped upon them in the past?" These and other questions need answering; I want to know, and I believe every colored American, who is thinking, wants to know.*

> Source: Neil A. Wynn. *The African American Experience during World War II*. Lanham, MD: Rowman & Littlefield Publishers, 2010. Print. 110.

Consider Your Audience

Adapt this passage for a different audience, such as your friends. Write a blog post conveying this same information for the new audience. How does your post differ from the original text and why?

BACK ON THE GROUND

After the war ended, Spann returned home to New Jersey. The military discharged many men, or released them from military service. Spann was discharged in 1946. He decided to join the US Army Reserve. The army reserve is a backup force that may be called on to fight in a conflict. Army reserve soldiers go back to their civilian lives. They can work or go to school. They do some military training each year to maintain their skills.

Spann wanted to continue flying. He tried to find a job with an airline. But the airlines

Some surviving Tuskegee Airmen and their families attended the New York City Veterans Day Parade in 2013.

35

would not hire him. He called other Black pilots who had also applied for pilot positions. None of them had gotten a job. They were not hired because they were African Americans.

Spann was forced to pursue a different career. He decided to attend the Newark College of Engineering. He worked in the evenings at a chemical company in New Jersey.

DESEGREGATING THE MILITARY

Many Black soldiers hoped they would find acceptance at home after serving abroad. But this was not the case. Segregation persisted. Black people still faced violence and discrimination. Some white people beat, arrested, and killed Black veterans.

President Harry S. Truman heard about attacks on Black veterans. In response, he signed Executive Order 9981 on July 26, 1948. This order desegregated the military. But Spann decided not to rejoin the service. He remembered a fellow pilot who was married. The pilot

AFRICAN AMERICANS IN THE MILITARY

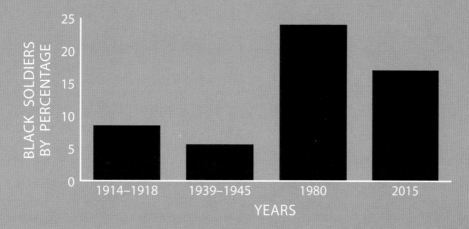

The graph above shows how the makeup of African Americans in the military changed from the early 1900s to 2015. How have these numbers changed over time? What do you think may be some reasons for these changes?

had died in Italy. Spann was married at this time. He worried about what would happen to his wife if he were killed in action. He did not want her to be lonely and grieving. He did not want her to have to support herself.

LATER LIFE AND LEGACY

To keep up his flying status in the reserve, Spann had to get in four hours of flight time each month. On weekends, he went to the airport that was closest to his house to try to get a plane. But often no planes were available on the weekends. Because he did not have a chance to fly, Spann decided to leave the reserve in 1961.

The 1950s and 1960s were the height of the American civil rights movement. This movement's goal was to help African Americans gain equal rights. Activists also fought racial discrimination. Some politicians listened and took action.

In 1961 President John F. Kennedy signed an order called Affirmative Action. It would increase the number of African Americans and other minorities in certain jobs. This would give them more job opportunities.

Spann, *second from left,* **and other Tuskegee Airmen were given the Congressional Gold Medal at a ceremony in 2007.**

At the time, Spann was working for a medical company. The company trained some of its African American employees to become medical sales representatives. Spann received this training. He also earned his real estate license. During these years, Spann had three children. He worked hard to support his family.

Spann worked as a medical sales representative until he retired. He continued working in real estate. He also became involved in Tuskegee Airmen Inc.

This organization creates programs to teach students many subjects, including math and science. As part of the organization, Spann visited schools, churches, and libraries. He talked about the airmen and their successes in Europe and at home.

Spann moved to McKinney, Texas, in 2006. He wanted to be closer to his daughter and his grandchildren. He died in McKinney on September 6, 2015. But his legacy and the legacy of the Tuskegee Airmen live on.

STRAIGHT TO THE
SOURCE

On July 14, 2011, Spann gave a presentation at a library in Allen, Texas. He talked about his experiences at home after returning from the war. He said,

> I successfully completed the missions in Europe and I came home. [I thought] I'm a flyer now, I can fly any kind of plane with an engine on it and two wings. . . . When I get home, I'm going to continue flying. I love flying. I can fly anything with an engine, and I can fly anywhere in the country. . . . [But] we found out that nobody got a job. Nobody Black got a job flying. And that was the most disappointing thing in my life that ever happened to me. My family could see it. I still feel bad about it.

Source: Calvin Spann. "Allen Public Library Presents: Tuskegee Airman Lt. Calvin Spann." *Swagit Productions*. Allen City Television, July 14, 2011. Web. Accessed May 16, 2019.

What's the Big Idea?
Take a close look at this passage. What is the main idea? How did discrimination continue to affect Spann and other African Americans after the war?

FAST FACTS

- Calvin Spann was born in New Jersey on November 28, 1924.

- Spann joined the Army Air Corps so he could learn to fly.

- Black pilots were not allowed to train with white pilots. Spann and other Black pilots trained at the Tuskegee Army Air Field in Tuskegee, Alabama. They became known as the Tuskegee Airmen.

- Spann flew as a bomber and reconnaissance escort with the 332nd Fighter Group. He participated in 26 missions.

- After World War II ended, Spann was discharged from the military. He tried to become an airline pilot, but airlines would not hire Black pilots.

- On July 26, 1948, President Harry S. Truman signed Executive Order 9981. This order desegregated the military.

- Spann joined the US Army Reserve, but he could not meet the requirements to keep up his flying status. He left the reserve and worked as a sales representative for a medical company.

- Spann spoke at libraries, schools, and churches to remind people about the airmen and their accomplishments.

- Spann died on September 6, 2015.

STOP AND THINK

Tell the Tale

Chapter One of this book talks about the Tuskegee Airmen's longest flight on a mission in 1945. Imagine you were a part of this mission. Write 200 words about your experience.

Dig Deeper

After reading this book, what questions do you still have about the Tuskegee Airmen? With an adult's help, find a few reliable sources that can help you answer your questions. Write a paragraph about what you learned.

Why Do I Care?

The Tuskegee Airmen had outstanding service records during World War II. Their contributions also led to changes at home. Think about the airmen's legacy. How might the United States be different today if they had not served?

GLOSSARY

bombardier
a member of a bomber crew who is responsible for sighting and releasing bombs

cadet
a student at a military school

civil rights
the rights guaranteed to all citizens of a nation or country

civilian
a person who is not serving in the military

discriminate
to treat a person or a group of people unjustly based on their race or other perceived differences

draft
a process by which people are chosen for military duty

meteorology
the study of Earth's weather and atmosphere

porter
a person who carries passengers' luggage on a train

radar
a device that sends out radio waves to find an object

segregation
the separation of people based on race or other factors

ONLINE
RESOURCES

To learn more about Calvin Spann and the Tuskegee Airmen, visit our free resource websites below.

Visit **abdocorelibrary.com** or scan this QR code for free Common Core resources for teachers and students, including vetted activities, multimedia, and booklinks, for deeper subject comprehension.

Visit **abdobooklinks.com** or scan this QR code for free additional online weblinks for further learning. These links are routinely monitored and updated to provide the most current information available.

LEARN
MORE

Smith, Sherri L. *Who Were the Tuskegee Airmen?* New York: Penguin Workshop, 2018.

Weatherford, Carole Boston. *You Can Fly: The Tuskegee Airmen.* New York: Atheneum Books for Young Readers, 2016.

ABOUT THE
AUTHORS

Duchess Harris, JD, PhD

Dr. Harris is a professor of American Studies at Macalester College and curator of the Duchess Harris Collection of ABDO books. She is also the coauthor of the titles in the collection, which features popular selections such as *Hidden Human Computers: The Black Women of NASA* and series including News Literacy and Being Female in America.

Before working with ABDO, Dr. Harris authored several other books on the topics of race, culture, and American history. She served as an associate editor for *Litigation News*, the American Bar Association Section of Litigation's quarterly flagship publication, and was the first editor in chief of *Law Raza*, an interactive online journal covering race and the law, published at William Mitchell College of Law. She has earned a PhD in American Studies from the University of Minnesota and a JD from William Mitchell College of Law.

Samantha S. Bell

Samantha S. Bell lives with her family in upstate South Carolina. She graduated from Furman University with a degree in history and a teaching certification in social studies. She is the author of more than 90 nonfiction books for children.

INDEX